THE PEOPLE OF POMPEII

By Pamela Rushby

Illustrated by Xiangyi Mo

Pearson Australia
(a division of Pearson Australia Group Pty Ltd)
707 Collins Street, Melbourne, Victoria 3008
PO Box 23360, Melbourne, Victoria 8012
www.pearson.com.au

First published 2010 by Pearson Australia
2020 2019 2018 2017
10 9 8 7 6 5 4 3 2 1

Publisher: Simone Calderwood
Illustrator: Xiangyi Mo
Editors: Lisa Warden and Sophie Ayerbe
Designer: Jennifer Johnston
Copyright & Pictures Editor: Helen Mammides
Project Editor: Aisling Coughlan
Production Controller: Claire Henry
Printed in Australia by the SOS Print + Media Group

ISBN 978 1 4425 2808 6

Pearson Australia Group Pty Ltd ABN 40 004 245 943

Contents

A Note from the Author

THOUSANDS OF YEARS AGO, in 79 CE, a volcano in Italy called Mount Vesuvius erupted violently and unexpectedly. The nearby Roman towns of Pompeii, Herculaneum (say *herk-you-LAY-nee-um*) and Stabiae (say *STAR-bee-ay*) were destroyed in the eruption, buried under either ashes or lava.

We have an eyewitness account of the eruption in a letter written by an eighteen-year-old boy, known as Pliny the Younger, who watched it happen. His uncle, Pliny the Elder, died in the eruption. The letter survived and it can be read today.

Twenty thousand people lived in the busy town of Pompeii. Many of them ran away and escaped. But about 2000 of them died, suffocated by the poisonous gases that poured from the volcano and then buried under the falling ash. When the eruption was over, the town was completely covered by almost three metres of ash and small rocks. It was forgotten for over 1600 years.

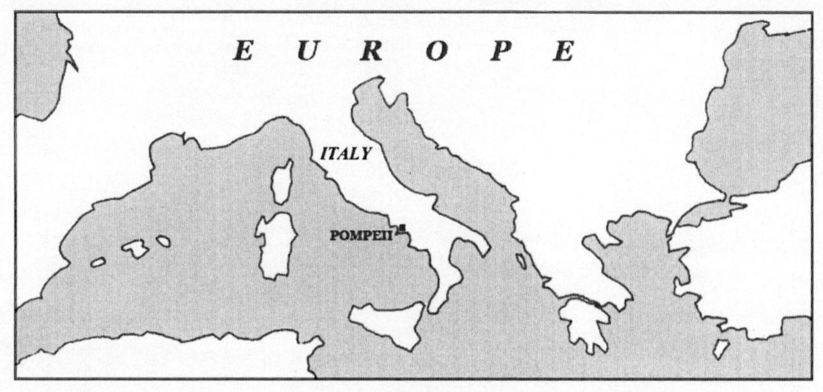

Then, from the mid-1700s, the town of Pompeii was rediscovered and archaeologists began to uncover its buildings. Today, you can walk through the streets of Pompeii again. They look just as they did when they were buried in 79 CE. It's like a time capsule of a Roman town: the buildings, the food, the streets, the artworks, the gardens—even the graffiti that had been scribbled on its walls.

And Mount Vesuvius is still there, looming over the town. It is still an active volcano today.

Pamela Rushby

Note: To find out how to say some of the Italian and Latin words in this book, go to the Pronunciation Guide on page 72.

Chapter 1

The World Holds Its Breath

THE AIR IN THE GARDEN grew suddenly and strangely still. It was as if the clouds drifting across the sky had frozen and the whole world held its breath for a second.

A moment later, the surface of the fish pond where Flavia had been dipping her fingers, trying to touch the fish, seemed to shiver. Ripples broke across its smooth surface and splashed at the edge of the pond. The fish dived abruptly to the bottom.

The glasses that Anilla, the slave woman, had just placed on the table shook and rattled. Anilla held the jug closer and put her hand out to steady the glasses.

"Oh, no!" Flavia cried.

But it wasn't the odd feeling in the air, or the strange rippling of the pond that had upset her. That often happened here in the Roman town of Pompeii—small earth tremors were common.

The air was still for another moment, and some plates rattled on the shelves in the kitchen, then everything was normal again.

There hadn't been a large earthquake in Pompeii for sixteen years—four years before Flavia was born. Then, many buildings in the town had been destroyed. But they had all been rebuilt, and no-one expected that such a severe earthquake would ever happen again.

No, it wasn't the tiny earth tremor that was upsetting Flavia, but that her father, Marcus, had just told her and her mother, Lucilla, that he would be going away soon on a trading journey.

"Oh," said Lucilla. "I see. And how long do you expect to be away?"

Marcus looked uncomfortable. "Rather a long time. I need to go to the East, as well as to the Baltic. We need more amber and silks.

The stock in the warehouses is getting low. It could be—"

He hesitated. He knew Lucilla and Flavia wouldn't like this.

"It could be months. Maybe six months. Maybe more."

"Six months!" said Flavia. "So long!"

"But that means you'll miss your niece Justina's wedding," said Lucilla. "And your nephew Lucius's coming-of-age celebration. They will be so disappointed if you're not there."

"That's just it," said Marcus. "That's why I have to go. Gaius can't go because it is his daughter who is getting married. Titus can't go because it's his son's coming-of-age celebration."

Gaius and Titus were Marcus's older brothers.

Justina was Gaius's daughter and Lucius was Titus's son. Marcus and his brothers were merchants, partners in a business that imported luxury goods such as silks, amber, spices and perfumes.

The three brothers journeyed to faraway lands to find these goods and bring them back to Pompeii.

They worked hard, and they had done very well out of their business. All three men owned large, new houses and their families lived in comfort. But if they were to continue living in comfort, it seemed that Marcus had to go away.

"Because my brothers have to stay in Pompeii," Marcus went on, "it has to be me who goes away this time. After all," he smiled at Flavia, "I don't expect you will be getting married in the next six months. Will you?"

"Married!" said Lucilla. "Certainly not. But we will have to start looking around for a suitable young man soon. Very soon."

She gave Marcus a severe look. "You've put off finding a husband for Flavia, and she's twelve now. We should have arranged it years ago. If we aren't careful, all the right sort of young men will be taken. You know that Justina has been promised for marriage since she was eight years old."

"I know, I know," Marcus said. "I just don't like the idea of losing our Flavia, I suppose. I promise to do something about arranging it as soon as I get back."

He reached out for one of the glasses that Anilla, the slave woman, had poured and passed it to Lucilla.

"While I'm away, why don't you have a look around and see if there's anyone who might be suitable? There should be plenty of young men at Justina's wedding and Lucius's coming-of-age celebration." He smiled at his daughter. "And, after all, we won't actually have to do anything about a wedding for Flavia for a couple of years yet."

"Wedding!" exclaimed Flavia. "I'd rather go to the East with you. Or Egypt—I'd love to go to Egypt!"

"Well, why not?" said Marcus. "Once I come back from this trading journey, and the warehouses are full again, we'll all go on a journey together. We can go to Egypt, if you like. The pyramids—now, they are something to see!

But, for now, what would you like me to bring back for you this time? Silks for some new tunics? An amber necklace? Perhaps a bracelet?"

"Yes, please!" cried Flavia, clapping her hands together.

Chapter 2

Marcus Goes Away

ONLY A WEEK LATER, Lucilla, Flavia and the servants and slaves stood at the door of their house to say goodbye to Marcus.

"There's no need to come to the dock with me," Marcus said. "It's too noisy and crowded there. Better to say goodbye here."

Flavia bit her lip. She hated her father going away for such a long time.

"No tears," Marcus said to her. "Remember, we'll go to Egypt when I get back! Now, you look after your mother." He turned to Anilla. "Anilla, I trust you to take care of them."

Anilla nodded. "I will, Master." Anilla had been with Lucilla before Lucilla and Marcus were married.

Marcus signalled to a slave to open the door in the high wall that led to the street.

Immediately, dust, noise and smells flooded in. Carts rattled over stone streets, donkeys brayed, people shouted about the goods they were selling. Street musicians played pipes, cymbals and tambourines. There was a lovely smell of baking bread. But there were also other smells, far less pleasant, where people had thrown rubbish into the street.

Marcus stepped carefully over the open drain in the middle of the street, turned around and waved once—and was gone.

The slave closed the door, and Lucilla and Flavia were left standing quietly at the entrance.

Flavia looked down at its mosaic floor.

It was a picture of a fierce watchdog, made up of thousands of tiny coloured tiles. Under the picture were the words *Cave Canem*, which meant "beware of the dog".

Flavia's eyes filled with tears. This was one of Marcus's jokes. Her father had a great sense of humour. When the house was being built, Marcus had asked for the dog mosaic to be put there "to scare away any thieves!" he'd said.

Her father had also ordered the mosaic floor in the dining room to be made to look like an unswept floor—as if the dinner guests had been throwing food scraps on the ground. So the floor was covered with mosaic pictures of chicken and fish bones, oyster shells, lobster claws and fruit stones. There was even a picture of a tiny mouse feeding on the scraps!

On the walls, Marcus had decided to have artists paint funny pictures of pygmies battling with storks. Lucilla had insisted, however, that the pictures included plenty of flowers, trees and fountains as well, so the pictures were pretty. You had to look quite hard to find the pygmies and storks.

Flavia looked for them now, as she and her mother walked from the front of the house through to the enclosed, private garden at the back. *When father comes home*, she thought, *and we go on our Egyptian journey together, maybe I'll see* real *pygmies*! *Or will I*?

"Where do pygmies come from?" she asked Lucilla. "Is it Africa or Egypt?"

Her mother wasn't sure. "Let's ask Syrus, the next time he comes to give you your lessons," she suggested. "Syrus will know."

Flavia had finished school just a few months ago. Now, a freed Greek slave, Syrus, came to teach her at home.

Lucilla looked at Flavia. "Do you miss going to school?" she asked.

Flavia thought about it. Most boys and girls in Pompeii went to school together, until they were eleven or twelve years old. From then on, girls were taught at home, while boys went on to study law, mathematics, philosophy or public speaking.

"I do miss seeing my friends every day," Flavia said. "But I see them when I go with you to the other ladies' houses. I don't miss the teachers though! Syrus is nice. And he knows about everything!"

"Well, perhaps we'll go the baths this afternoon," Lucilla said. "I'm sure some of your friends will be there—and mine, too." *And*, she thought, *I'll keep my eyes open for the mothers with sons who might be a good match for Flavia*!

Chapter 3

A Wish Comes True

From then on, every time Lucilla went out, she kept her eyes open for a suitable husband for Flavia. She looked carefully at the mothers she and Flavia met when they went shopping. At the shoemaker's shop, while ordering new shoes, she made a point of chatting to another customer, Valeria.

Lucilla didn't like Valeria very much, but she knew Valeria had sons, which meant it might be worth getting to know her better. So Lucilla chatted to Valeria while the shoemaker measured their feet, and the shoemaker's wife brought out some of the latest styles from Rome for them to see.

"Yes, very nice," said Lucilla, admiring the shoes. "I'll have a pair in blue, and a pair in red. And Flavia needs several pairs too." She looked meaningfully at Valeria. "She's growing up so fast. Just think, twelve years old already! Only a few years and we'll be thinking about a marriage!"

Lucilla also looked carefully at all the young men who went to Justina's wedding. Lucilla and Flavia wore their best clothes for the occasion—smooth, flowing tunics made of silk from the East, and wraps of the finest wool. Anilla did Flavia's hair in soft, simple curls, and she piled Lucilla's hair up high and covered her head in tight ringlets.

At Justina's house, Flavia and her cousins

watched as Justina placed her childhood dresses and toys on the altar as an offering to the gods of the household. Now that she was getting married, she was grown up—she wouldn't need them any more.

The girls helped Justina dress in a white tunic and a saffron-coloured veil, and put a wreath of flowers on her head.

"I'm so nervous!" moaned Justina. "What if something goes wrong?"

"Nothing will go wrong," the girls told her. "You look beautiful!"

Justina's family walked with her and her parents to the bridegroom's house. While musicians played melodies, the family sang and handed out gifts of nuts to children they passed along the way.

When they arrived at her new home, Justina rubbed the door with olive oil, then she was lifted over the threshold—because if she stumbled, it would be very unlucky. Her bridegroom gave her a flaming torch to light the fire in her new house.

Now it would be Justina's job to run this household, and she would be expected to do it as well as her mother and mother-in-law ran theirs.

"I don't want to do that yet," Flavia whispered to one of her cousins, as they joined in the feast that followed.

"Me neither," her cousin whispered back. "It's a good thing we've got a few years before we'll be expected to get married!"

A few weeks later, Lucilla and Flavia went to Lucius's coming-of-age ceremony. They rode to the centre of the town, the forum, in chairs carried by slaves. There, Lucius took off his *bulla*, the protective charm he'd worn around his neck since he was a baby, and laid it on the altar to the god Bacchus.

Lucius made an offering of honey cakes to the god. His hair was cut into a man's hairstyle, and a barber gave him his first shave.

Flavia and her cousins giggled together. Lucius might be considered a man and a Roman citizen now, but his voice still went up and down as he spoke, squeaking and croaking.

Lucius gave the girls a look as he put on his man's toga. *I'm not so grown up that I can't deal with you lot later!* his look said.

Then all the excitement of family events was over and it seemed to Flavia that there was a long, long time to wait before Marcus came home.

"How long?" she asked Lucilla. "How long now?"

"Well, let's see," said her mother patiently. She began to count. "He's been away for five weeks..."

It was a hot morning. The air felt heavy, and the sky was a strange brassy colour. Perhaps there'd be a storm later. Lucilla and Flavia were sitting in the garden, hoping to find a breeze, but there was none.

Flavia looked up. Over the garden wall, over the roofs of the houses, she could see the mountain that stood over Pompeii. She could see small houses and fields on its slopes, so far away they were just white dots and green squares.

"...so it will be weeks yet, I'm afraid," Lucilla said.

Flavia sighed. Weeks! Weeks filled with nothing but ordinary days before she could even think of Egypt.

Anilla came into the garden carrying a jug and glasses, and some fruit and honey cakes. "You had better have something to eat and drink now," she said to Flavia. "Syrus will be here for your lessons soon."

Flavia sighed again. "I don't feel like lessons today. I wish something more interesting than food and lessons and visits to other families' houses would happen," she said.

Anilla smiled. "Be careful what you wish for," she said. "Your wish might come true. And you might find you do not like it."

And then, at that moment, Flavia's wish did come true. In a way they could never have imagined.

Chapter 4

The Mountain Explodes

THE AIR grew suddenly and strangely still. The fish pond rippled and the glasses that Anilla had placed on the table rattled—just as they always did. But this time the earth did not shiver and then settle down again. This time it kept moving.

Lucilla, Flavia and Anilla grabbed the garden table to steady themselves as the ground heaved and rocked under their feet.

In the street outside, there was a crash. Someone shouted, "Look out, the wall is collapsing!" There was another crash, and a confused babble of voices.

The earth grew still again. Lucilla reached out for Flavia and held her. "Well! That was a big one!" she said, trying to reassure her daughter.

"I think it's over now, Mistress," said Anilla. "I think—"

And then a roar, the loudest sound any of them had ever heard, ripped the sky apart. They pressed their hands to their ears, as the noise went on and on and on. There seemed to be nothing in the world but this huge, deafening roar, all around them.

Flavia looked up in terror. What was happening? There was the mountain she had been gazing at, only minutes ago. But now the mountain had completely changed. Its top had gone. Simply disappeared. Above it, a great dark cloud was shooting into the sky, rising higher and higher, faster than a man could run or a horse could gallop, first a straight column like the trunk of a giant tree, then spreading out, like a tree's branches.

"Look!" yelled Flavia. "Look at the mountain!"

The servants and slaves had come running and staggering into the garden. They all stared up at the mountain.

Lucilla screamed. Anilla, her face pale as milk, put an arm around her.

And the great dark cloud climbed higher and higher, with lightning and fire flashing around its edges.

"The gods!"

"It's the gods! They're angry!"

"The gods are destroying the earth!"

"What do we do?"

The servants and slaves huddled together. No-one could take their eyes off the cloud.

"Mistress! Flavia! Are you all right? Was anyone hurt?" Syrus had arrived. "I was on my way here when it happened," he panted. "I ran—the streets are full of rubble—"

"Syrus!" Flavia caught his arm. "Syrus! What is it? Is it—is it the gods?"

Syrus glanced at the servants and slaves. He lowered his voice. It didn't do to speak against the gods. "The gods? Perhaps. But I think it's a natural happening. A volcano."

"A volcano? The god Vulcan is punishing us?" gasped Lucilla.

"No, not a god," Syrus said. "A volcano is—" He stopped. This was no time for lectures and lessons.

He looked at Lucilla. "Mistress, you need to leave. Get away from the town. Get as far away as you can."

"What is going to happen?" Flavia shook Syrus's arm.

"Who knows? But right under Mount Vesuvius is not the place to stay," Syrus said.

"I'm leaving now. You should do the same."

"Leave?" Lucilla cried. "Where should we go?"

But Syrus had already left the garden.

The servants and slaves had heard Syrus too. One by one, they began to slip away. Flavia watched them go, but she didn't try to stop them. Syrus had said to go.

Soon it was just Flavia, Lucilla and Anilla left in the garden.

"We should go too," Flavia urged her mother. "Look! Look what's happening!"

The dark cloud had risen even higher above the mountain, so high into the air that it started to blot out the sun.

And now, at last, a breeze came. But the wind was pushing the cloud towards Pompeii. It rolled towards the town like a huge breaking wave moving towards the shore.

The air in front of Flavia's eyes grew thick and misty. She held her hand out. It wasn't mist. Tiny fragments of ash and rock began to collect in her palm. "Look!" she said to Anilla. "Feel this! It's hot!"

Lucilla was still frozen, staring up at the mountain with the lightning and fire silhouetting it against the great cloud.

"Mistress! We must go!" Anilla took Lucilla by the shoulders.

At last, Lucilla seemed to make up her mind. "Yes, we must," she said. "To the harbour. A boat. That's what we need—a boat."

They ran into the house, towards the door that led out to the street. Lucilla disappeared into her bedroom. She came out with a basket and handed it to Anilla. Flavia glanced into it. Jewellery and a purse of money. Anilla had already gathered up thick, hooded cloaks for all of them.

"It's getting so dark," whispered Flavia.

"We can still see," Anilla tried to reassure her. "We'll be able to reach the harbour. It's not far."

Anilla opened the door to the street. She took a sudden step backwards.

"Oh!" she gasped.

CHAPTER 5

WE MUST GET AWAY!

OUTSIDE THE DOOR, many of the houses in the street were on fire. The flames gave light in the growing darkness. And what Flavia saw, by the light of the flames, was that the street was packed with people, jammed with people, and everyone was running and screaming.

It looked as if all Pompeii's 20 000 citizens were crowded into this one narrow street. Some were heading towards the harbour, but others were running in the other direction, pushing against the crowd, and blocking the street even more.

"The ocean! The ocean has pulled back!" they shouted. "The boats can't get out! Turn back!"

While Flavia watched, a woman holding a baby stumbled and fell. In a moment, she had disappeared under hundreds of running feet.

Anilla slammed the door shut and barred it. "Not that way," she said.

"Perhaps we should wait," said Flavia desperately. "If we shelter here, surely it will stop…"

But the darkness only grew deeper. Lucilla, Flavia and Anilla stayed in the house for a while, but then they went back to the garden. Although they could barely see the mountain any more, they could not keep their eyes off it.

The air began to smell bad, and smoke from

the burning houses made it hard to breathe. Hot ash and small stones fell faster and faster.

It's like rain, Flavia thought, *but a strange rain that does not run away or soak into the ground*. It began to pile up, on the ground and on roofs, and the piles grew higher and higher.

In the garden, the ash and stones reached above Flavia's ankles. Flavia looked up at the sky. *It must be almost night by now*, she thought, *but there's no way to tell*. The town was covered in a thick, choking blackness. There were no stars in the sky.

The falling stones were growing bigger. Lucilla, Flavia and Anilla stepped back into the shelter of the garden verandah. Then, with a crack, a section of the verandah roof collapsed under the weight of the falling rocks.

"We must get away," Lucilla said. "It's not safe here."

Flavia looked again at the exploding mountain. Despite the darkness, she could see its slopes were covered with patches of fire, and the boiling cloud above it was an angry, livid red.

The bad smell in the air was getting worse.

"We'll try again," said Anilla.

She unbarred the door to the street, but she couldn't open it. Ash had piled up on the other side. Anilla pushed and heaved until she forced it open.

She looked out. The street seemed to be quieter, but it was so dark that it was hard to tell.

"I can't see," called Anilla. "We need lamps." She turned back to the house to get them.

Flavia took a step out into the street. As soon as she left the shelter of the house, a falling rock hit her cheek. It hurt. She put up her hand and felt blood.

If bigger rocks fall, Flavia thought, *we could be knocked unconscious*. "Cushions!" she said. "We need cushions! We can hold them over our heads."

They wrapped themselves in the thick cloaks, tied cushions to their heads with belts, and held up their lamps.

In the dim light of the lamps, they looked at each other. Even now, they could manage small smiles at how ridiculous they looked.

"Let's go!" said Flavia. And they stepped out into the street.

Chapter 6

We'll Be Safe Here

In seconds, Flavia, Lucilla and Anilla had no idea where they were. Walls had fallen. Roofs had collapsed. Rubble lay in the street. There were fewer people now, but the ones who were there all seemed to be lost, stumbling from one side of the street to the other, wading through the layer of ash and stones that grew higher and higher.

Flavia, Lucilla and Anilla coughed and choked and tried to shield their faces from the foul-smelling air with their cloaks.

"Where are we?" gasped Lucilla.

"I don't know," said Anilla. "But keep going! We must keep going!"

Some people had not kept going. They had fallen at the side of the street, arms stretched above their heads, cloaks and scarves pulled over their faces.

Already the ash was collecting on top of them, covering them. And they seemed to be still, so still.

We're not going to get away, Flavia thought numbly. *We won't get out of the town.*

She tried to take a deep breath, and choked as the air seemed to burn right down her throat and into her lungs.

It would be so easy to sit down and give up, she thought. But Anilla forced them to go on.

"The town gates," she said. "We must find the gates. If we can get out into the country..."

But they had no idea which way the gates were. They waded through the ash, feeling their way along walls, stopping at corners to see if they could recognise the streets around them. Lucilla began to slow down, clutching at walls to support herself, falling behind.

"I'm all right," she called when Flavia turned around to see where she was. "Keep going! I'll catch up!" Flavia and Anilla looked at each other. They knew she wouldn't.

Then they turned a corner and suddenly Flavia knew where they were. "We're near the forum! It's the shoemaker's shop!" she said. "Look!" She stepped into the doorway of the shop.

"Then we have quite a long way to go." Anilla bit her lip. "Well..." she straightened up. "At least we know which way to go now."

Lucilla caught up with them, coughing and gasping. Anilla looked at her anxiously. "We'll rest here for just a moment," she said.

They all leaned against the walls of the shop and tried to take deep breaths.

"Who's there?"

The voice came from under their feet. They all jumped in shock. Lucilla fell to her knees, and Anilla tried to catch her.

"Who's there, I say?"

A head appeared from a door in the corner, near the floor. Beside it was a hand holding a lamp. Flavia started to laugh. "It's the shoemaker!" she said.

The shoemaker stared at them. "Mistress Lucilla? Anilla? It is Anilla, isn't it?"

"Yes, yes, it's Anilla," Anilla said. "We're trying to get out of town, we were lost—"

The shoemaker shook his head. "You won't get out tonight. You'd better stay here with us. We're in the storeroom, under the shop. Come and shelter with us, and in the morning we'll get out of town." He beckoned them towards the door.

Slowly, they followed him. Under the floor, in the storeroom, was the shoemaker's family—his wife, his two little girls, even the family dog. They had lamps and food. They looked frightened but they were snug in there.

Flavia looked at the shoemaker gratefully. "Thank you," she said. "Thank you so much."

She pulled the cushion from her head and took off her cloak. She smiled at the two little girls and their mother. She bent and patted the dog.

"You see?" the shoemaker said. "You'll be safe in here with us. Come in, come in. Are you hungry? Now we'll all settle down here, and in the morning we'll see what's what. You'll see, we'll all be safe in here. Absolutely safe."

CHAPTER 7

1800 YEARS LATER

ALMOST ONE THOUSAND and eight hundred years later, in 1863, a girl called Maria walked down a street in Pompeii with her uncle, Carlo.This was nothing like the Pompeii that Flavia knew. This Pompeii was a low hill. In places, men were digging in the earth. Other men were carrying earth and rubble and rocks away in large wicker baskets, balanced on their shoulders.

As the men dug, they uncovered the roofs and walls of houses and shops. In some places, they had uncovered the buildings down to their floors, and they had opened up the cobbled streets that lay between the houses.

Maria and Carlo were walking along one of these streets. There were no workmen near them—this part of the street had been cleared and the men had moved on. They could hear their voices in the distance, but where they were walking there was only silence.

"It's… it's like a town of ghosts," Maria said. The sun was warm on her head and shoulders, but she shivered. "So quiet! No people! Just houses—without people."

"It wouldn't have been quiet," her uncle said. "Far from it. Pompeii would have been a very busy town. Lots of people, lots of carts and donkeys in the street.

"See that?" he continued. "That was a public fountain. People went there every day to get their water. And that? That was a public latrine—a toilet. See the drain that carried the waste away? They didn't use toilet paper then, you know. They used sponges, on the end of sticks."

"Sponges?" asked Maria, horrified. "And you mean they used them over and over? And left them for the next person? Ugh!"

Uncle Carlo changed the subject. It seemed as if he'd suddenly realised that Maria's mother might not want her knowing too much about ancient toilets.

"And over here," he said quickly, "we think that was a shop that sold ready-cooked food. See these big jars, set into the counter? They held the hot food."

Maria stopped to look at some open-fronted buildings. "Were these shops too?"

"Probably they all were. But above them, people would have lived in apartments.

We know one shop was a bakery, because there was some bread left in the shop. It was still there. Just think of it, Maria! Still there after all this time! Bread that's nearly 1800 years old!"

Maria smiled at her uncle. She liked him very much. He was a lot younger than Maria's father. He'd come to live with her family three years ago, when he got this job, helping to excavate the town of Pompeii.

Maria remembered the day he'd come to see them, after he'd had an interview with Signor Giuseppe Fiorelli, the archaeologist who had just been put in charge of the excavations at Pompeii.

"I got the job!" Carlo had shouted, halfway down the street. Maria, her parents and all the neighbours had come out to see what all the noise was about. "I got the job! I'm going to work with Signor Fiorelli!" He grabbed Maria's hands and danced her around the street.

Maria's parents took him inside and they sat down to hear all about it.

"Signor Fiorelli is a real scientist!" Carlo said. "He showed me some of the records he's been keeping, and how he works. He's divided the town into sections, and he's uncovering each of them properly, one by one, keeping detailed notes on everything he finds. Not like all those people, years ago, who were just after artworks and treasure! Do you know, they used to knock their way through walls and destroy paintings and mosaics? Would you believe it?"

Maria's parents smiled. They were happy to see Carlo so excited and to see how proud he was to have been offered this job.

"So, now I need to find a place to live," Carlo said.

Maria's mother was shocked. "You will not! You'll live with us, of course. For as long as you like, for as long as you're working here, I insist."

"But I can't do that," Carlo said. "I'll be in your way."

"You're family," said Maria's father. "Of course you'll live here."

Every day since he had come to live with them, Carlo had come home and told Maria and her parents about new discoveries that had been made. A beautiful statue, a fountain, a new painting. Maria loved hearing about all the things they'd found. She wished she could go and see them. *Pompeii must be a wonderful place!* she thought.

Chapter 8

A Visit to Pompeii

THEN, A FEW DAYS AGO, Carlo came home from work and told them about a mosaic they'd just finished uncovering.

"It's at the entrance to a house that looks as if it belonged to a wealthy family," he said. "It's a picture of a fierce guard dog. And it has the words *Cave Canem*—beware of the dog—written under it." He laughed. "I really like that! Someone had a good sense of humour!"

"Oh, I'd love to see that," Maria said. Then she bit her lip. Her mother had told her she wasn't to ask Uncle Carlo if she could go to see the buried city. Signor Fiorelli wouldn't want little girls around, her mother had said. Carlo might get into trouble if he took her. Maria looked guiltily at her mother. Her mother shook her head at her.

"Well, what a good idea!" Carlo said. "I don't know why I didn't think of it before! I'll ask Signor Fiorelli tomorrow. I'm sure he'll say yes. He loves it when people are interested in Pompeii!"

He looked at Maria's mother. "Why are you shaking your head like that?" he asked.

So, this morning, Maria got ready to see Pompeii with Uncle Carlo. She was wearing her best white dress that she wore to go to Mass on Sundays. Maria's mother had washed it and starched it and ironed it until it was as crisp as a biscuit. She'd told Maria to put on her best white stockings and shine her black leather boots, too.

"You must look as if you've been brought

up properly, if you're going to meet Signor Fiorelli!" she said.

Maria scratched her neck where the starched frill of her dress was making her itch, but she didn't say anything. If she complained, she might be told she should stay at home.

When Uncle Carlo came to the house to collect her at lunch time, he stared at the white dress and grinned. But he didn't say anything until they were well away from the house. Then he laughed.

"I can't imagine what you'll look like when you get home," he said. "An excavation site is no place for a white dress and stockings! Well, we'll do our best to keep you clean."

And now here they were, right in the middle of the ancient town, looking at a row of shops where people had baked bread and sold bread and come to buy bread so many years ago.

But what had happened to those people? Maria wondered. She and Uncle Carlo had walked down so many streets, and seen so many buildings, but there had been no sign of the people who'd lived in Pompeii.

Some workmen walked past, carrying baskets of earth and rubble on their shoulders. They looked at Maria curiously. *I suppose not many children visit here*, Maria thought.

But then Uncle Carlo called out to them, "Hello! This is my niece, Maria!" and the workmen grinned and called "Hello!" back.

Following them was a man wearing a big straw hat. He had a bundle of papers under his arm. "That's Signor Fiorelli," whispered Uncle Carlo. "Come on, let's say hello to him."

Signor Fiorelli stopped and smiled at them. "Is this your niece, Carlo?" he asked. "Maria, isn't it? So, what do you think of Pompeii, Maria?"

"Pompeii is wonderful!" said Maria. "The houses, and the shops, and the fountain—"

She'd been really interested in the public toilets, with rows of holes in a long marble seat and a drain running underneath it, but she supposed she'd better not talk about toilets to Signor Fiorelli.

"And Uncle Carlo is going to show me the mosaic of the dog that guards the house!"

"Ah, yes," said Signor Fiorelli. "That's one of my favourites, too. And do you know, we've been uncovering the frescoes—the wall paintings—in that house, and they have pictures of pygmies battling with storks. Amazing! Ask your uncle to show you that, too."

He started to walk away. "Have a lovely day, Maria."

But Maria had something she wanted to ask. "Signor Fiorelli—"

Signor Fiorelli turned back. “Yes?”

“The people,” said Maria. “Where are the people who lived here? They had lovely houses, and lots of shops and fountains and—and everything—” She managed to stop herself saying “toilets”. “But where are the people?”

“Gone,” said Uncle Carlo. “They all ran away when the volcano erupted.”

“All of them?” said Maria.

“All of them,” said Uncle Carlo.

But Signor Fiorelli was watching her. “Do you know, Maria, that’s something I’ve been asking myself,” he said. “No people. It’s strange, isn’t it? Surely not everyone escaped.”

He looked thoughtful. “There must have been old people, or sick people, or people who were injured when the volcano erupted, who wouldn’t have found it easy to get away. But just look at how many buildings and streets we’ve uncovered! And we’ve found no bodies, no skeletons, no remains of people at all.”

Signor Fiorelli thoughtfully stared out over the town. “Yes, it’s very strange. Very strange indeed.”

He stood thinking for another moment. "Well, I mustn't keep you away from the guard dog mosaic and the pygmy fresco," he said at last.

Maria bobbed a little curtsey, as her mother had told her she should. "Thank you for letting me visit, Signor Fiorelli," she said.

Another man had come up behind Signor Fiorelli and was waiting to talk to him. With another smile at Maria, Signor Fiorelli turned to look at the papers the man was carrying. "Yes, Angelo?" he said.

"I thought you'd like to know we've dug down into the cellar of that shop near the forum," the man said. "We've come across another one of those odd holes. You know, those hollows under the ground we find now and then."

"Yes," said Signor Fiorelli. "So there's one in the cellar, is there? I'll come and have a look." He started to walk off, then stopped and looked back at Carlo and Maria. "It's on your way, Carlo. Why don't you come, too? Maria might find it interesting."

They walked up the street together. In this part of Pompeii, the buildings were still being uncovered. Some of them were still buried in the earth. In some places, it looked as if no buildings had ever stood there at all.

"How did anyone ever know there was a town here, under the earth?" Maria asked.

"In the years after the eruption, people knew for a while," Signor Fiorelli told her. "When the eruption was over, Pompeii was buried under ash and rocks, about as deep as the height of two men. We imagine people who had lived here came back and dug, trying to find their houses and their possessions. But they would have kept striking pockets of poisonous gas under the earth, and some of them probably died.

"So it was too dangerous, and they gave up and moved away, and Pompeii was left alone. Grass and plants covered up the hill that was left. The local country people have always called the hill *la cività*—the city—but everyone soon forgot there actually had been a town here once."

"What reminded them?" asked Maria curiously.

"Well, over the years, people digging in the area for one reason or another—perhaps digging a well—might have come across part of an old building, or a vase or dish, or a statue.

"But no-one was really interested, not until just over a hundred years ago. Then, people started being interested in things from the past. But they were looking for treasure, such as artworks, statues and vases. And they didn't care at all how they got them. They dug tunnels and shafts, and they smashed through walls and ceilings and ruined frescoes and mosaics."

"That's terrible!" said Maria.

"I agree," said Signor Fiorelli."But later, the buried city—as people had begun to call it, started to become a place that people wanted to visit and look at. So the excavators were more careful. They found many more buildings, such as the barracks where gladiators lived, and a temple to the goddess Isis, and a theatre."

"But it wasn't until Signor Fiorelli was put in charge of the excavations that things were really done properly!" said Angelo. "Signor Fiorelli was appointed by the King of Italy himself, you know, Victor Emmanuel the Second!"

"Yes, well, never mind that." Signor Fiorelli looked embarrassed. "Ah, is this the shop, Angelo?"

"Yes," said Angelo. "The hole is in the cellar. We've cleared enough room so we can all go down to see."

Signor Fiorelli leapt down into the space under the floor of the shop. He bent down to look more closely at the small hole that had appeared in the cellar's floor. "Yes, I see," he said. He slid his hand into the hole and felt around. "Yes, it's quite a large hollow," he said. "Now what can these things be?" He looked up. "Maria, would you like to come and see?"

Maria looked at the dusty, ashy hole, and at her white dress and stockings. She knew she'd get filthy down there.

Then she thought, *Oh, for goodness' sake! I'm being invited by the director of the excavations of Pompeii to look at something that's just been discovered, and I'm worrying about my stockings?*

She jumped down into the hole.

Chapter 9

Hollows in the Earth

"**THERE**," said Signor Fiorelli. "You see how we've got a very small hole here? Well, the hollow underneath is bigger, much bigger than the hole. And it goes off in this direction, and in that direction, and it's quite deep."

Maria looked at it. "Can I put my hand in?" she asked. "Can I feel it?"

"Yes, of course," said Signor Fiorelli. "Gently, though."

Maria dropped to her knees and slid her hand into the hollow. She ran her fingers this way and that. She couldn't touch the bottom of the hollow. She leaned over further. She still couldn't touch the bottom.

Oh, bother it! she thought. *Bother white dresses!* And she lay flat on her stomach, in the ash and earth, and ran her fingers carefully around the hollow.

Now she could touch the bottom of the hollow. She ran her hand this way and that. It felt... it felt like... surely it couldn't be... But there was a rounded shape at one end, and two long shapes stretched above it, and then, at the other end, two more long shapes.

Maria closed her eyes, and felt the whole shape again. Then she looked up at Signor Fiorelli, with ash all over her face. "I think it's a person," she said.

"A what?" asked Uncle Carlo.

"A person," said Maria.

"But it's a hole, not a body!" said Angelo. He looked confused.

"Yes, I know," said Maria.

She tried to explain. “But it still feels like the shape of a person. Like a person was there, but they’ve gone now.”

Signor Fiorelli knelt down. “May I?” he said. Maria moved over and Signor Fiorelli lay flat on his stomach in the ash and earth, and felt around the hollow. He got up. He stared at the hole. He walked a few steps, then back. He stared at the hole again.

Then he said, “Angelo, Carlo, please fetch some buckets. And water. And plaster of Paris. And bring back some men to do some mixing and shovelling.”

Maria sat down on a pile of earth to watch.

When the men came back, they set to work, mixing a white powder with water until it was a thick liquid, then pouring it slowly into the hole. Signor Fiorelli watched every movement.

“Slowly, slowly,” he kept saying. “Very slowly! We don’t want air bubbles in there!”

The men mixed and poured, mixed and poured, until the white liquid was level with the top of the small hole. Then they began to pack up their tools.

"What happens now?" asked Maria.

"Now, we wait," said Signor Fiorelli. "It will take time for the plaster to harden and set. In a day or so, we'll remove the earth around the hollow, and see what we've got in there."

"What do you think it will be?" asked Maria.

"I'm not sure," said Signor Fiorelli. "But it will be very, very interesting to find out!"

Three days later, Uncle Carlo came home from work with an invitation for Maria to visit the excavation site again.

"Again?" said Maria's mother. "I don't think so! Look at the state she came home in last time! Her dress filthy! Her stockings ruined!"

"But it's very important," pleaded Uncle Carlo. "Signor Fiorelli has something he especially wants to show her. A surprise. And he's invited you, too—the whole family."

It took some time, but at last Maria's mother agreed. After all, not everyone got an invitation to visit Pompeii. And this time, she'd be there to make sure Maria stayed clean!

Maria's mother need not have worried, because they weren't going to crawl in holes under the ground this time.

This time, they were taken to a workroom where things that had been found in the excavations were stored. There were large pottery storage jars, kitchen utensils, some statues and vases. And a large shape, covered with a cloth, lying on a table in the middle of the workroom.

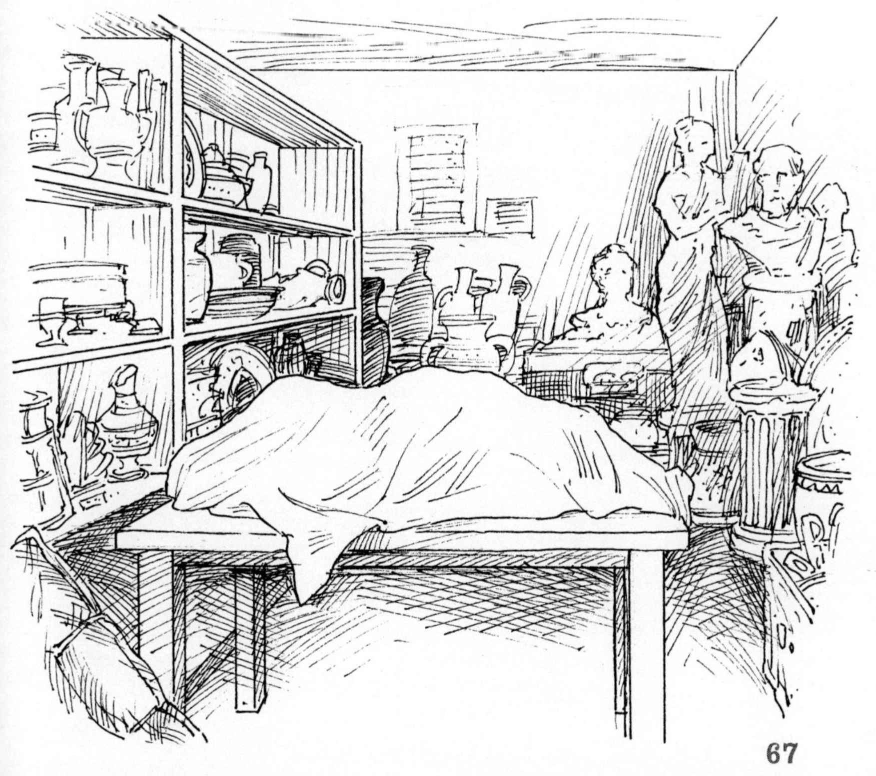

Maria's eyes were drawn straight to it. "Is this it?" she asked.

"This is it," nodded Signor Fiorelli. "This is what we found when we removed the earth from around the plaster cast we'd made." He paused.

"Why don't you take the cloth off, Maria?"

Slowly Maria stepped forward and took the edge of the cloth in her hand. She couldn't wait to see what was under it—but she'd be so disappointed if it wasn't what she thought it might be.

She pulled the cloth off.

Chapter 10

The People of Pompeii

EVERYONE GASPED. Lying on the table was a girl. A pure white shape of a girl in plaster of Paris. She looked about twelve years old, the same age as Maria. She was lying on her side. Her arms were flung above her head, as if she had been trying to hide her face with her arms.

She had been wearing a long tunic and sandals. Her long hair was tied in a simple bun at the base of her neck. Every detail of her dress and her body was there, imprinted in the plaster of Paris.

Maria stared at her. A girl about her own age. A girl who had been trying to escape from the volcano, but who had not made it. Slowly she put out her hand and gently touched the girl's cheek.

"She would have died from suffocation," said Signor Fiorelli softly. "The poisonous gases would have killed her, as she tried to hide in the cellar. And then the ash came, and covered her up. Over time, her body decayed, but it left her shape in the hardened ash. She would have looked just as you see her here."

"And that's not all," said Angelo. "There were other people in the cellar. We found more holes, and we filled them with plaster of Paris, too. There were two women near the girl. And a little bit further away, a man and a woman and two small children. We even found a dog."

But Maria was still looking at the girl. What must it have been like, she wondered, to have lived in this town so many years ago? How would this girl have felt, when she saw the mountain explode and the dark cloud begin to fall on her? Did she know she was going to die? Or did she still think, even up to her last moment, that she would be able to escape?

Could there be other buried people in Pompeii? Surely these couldn't be the only ones! There must be more to find here, much, much more. More buildings, more houses, more streets. More people.

She turned to Signor Fiorelli. "Signor," she asked. "Can girls become archaeologists?"

Signor Fiorelli smiled at her. "I'm sure they can, Maria," he said.

Pronunciation Guide

Here is a guide to help you say some of the Italian and Latin words and names that appear in this book:

Bacchus	*BACK-us*
Cave Canem	*CAR-way CAR-nem*
città	*chi-VEE-ta*
Fiorelli	*FEE-or-el-ee*
Giuseppe	*jew-ZEH-peh*
Herculaneum	*herk-you-LAY-nee-um*
Pompeii	*pom-PAY*
Signor	*seen-YAW*
Stabiae	*STAR-bee-ay*
Vesuvius	*veh-SOO-vee-us*